ANDY WARHOL

ediciones polígrafa

masterpieces
ANDY WARHOL

© 2005 Ediciones Polígrafa, S.A.
Balmes, 54. E-08007 Barcelona
www.edicionespoligrafa.com

Reproductions copyright © Andy Warhol, VEGAP, Barcelona 2005
© Text: María Vera Pachón
Translation: Alberto Curotto (biography: Sue Brownbridge)
Color separation: Format Digital (Barcelona)
Printed and bound at Mateu Cromo (Madrid)

Available in USA and Canada through D.A.P./Distributed Art Publishers
155 Sixth Avenue, 2nd Floor, New York, N.Y. 10013
Tel: (212) 627–1999 Fax: (212) 627–9484

ISBN: 84-343-1070-8
Dep. legal: B. 36.769 - 2005 (Printed in Spain)

CONTENTS

7 ANDY WARHOL: MORE THAN A POP ARTIST

11 ANDY WARHOL, 1928–1987

16 SELECTED BIOGRAPHY

18 SUCCESS IN NEW YORK

25 ART AS FORMULA

31 AT THE SUPERMARKET

43 REPORTS OF DEATH

55 WARHOL AS COURT PAINTER

65 ARCHETYPAL FORMS

78 LIST OF WORKS

SELF-PORTRAIT, 1966.
Acrylic paint and silkscreen
ink on canvas, 55.9 x 55.9 cm

ANDY WARHOL: MORE THAN A POP ARTIST

Andy Warhol has been called a mirror of his age. And indeed, Warhol's oeuvre—from his early graphic work to his exaltation of such commonplace items as Campbell's Soup cans to his celebrity to his seven-hour-long film of the Empire State Building—closely reflects the America of his time. For the artist's critics, his work constitutes the quintessential paradigm of the frivolousness and banality of that period. To be sure, Warhol intentionally cultivated a somewhat trivial image, one that he reinforced through many oft-quoted maxims, perhaps most notably his assertion that "If you want to know all about Andy Warhol just look at the surface: of my paintings and films and me, and there I am. There's nothing behind it." Yet few artists have had a greater impact on the world of art, and even fewer have ever achieved the kind of personal celebrity that Warhol enjoyed.

Indeed, Andy Warhol can be viewed as the perfect embodiment of the American Dream, the self-made man who successfully overcomes an impoverished upbringing to become a millionaire. Warhol personifies a new type of star, at once creator, producer, actor, and—last but not least—brilliant businessman. In fact, for Warhol, "Being good in business is the most fascinating kind of art," according to another of his famous aphorisms.

POP ART VS. ABSTRACT EXPRESSIONISM

Andy Warhol almost single-handedly modernized our aesthetic tradition. As far as both themes and mediums are concerned, Warhol was at the origin, or at least he became a symbol of a

say "Pepsi please"
CLOSE COVER BEFORE STRIKING

momentous transformation in contemporary painting. Even without almost ever resorting to ready-mades—he did indeed sign some cans of Campbell's Soup—Warhol challenged, more than any other Pop artist, the traditional conventions pertaining to the uniqueness, authenticity, and authorship of the work of art. He completed the process of dissolution of easel painting that had been initiated by the Abstract Expressionists, whose break with tradition was admittedly not as radical as Warhol's. Unlike such idealistic artists as Jackson Pollock, Franz Kline, Mark Rothko, or Barnett Newman, who had a profound veneration for the innermost world of consciousness, Warhol was obsessed by concreteness, the material world, that is, visible and tangible objects.

CLOSE COVER BEFORE STRIKING (PEPSI-COLA). 1962. Warhol has transformed a matchbox into a painterly work simply by enlarging its size, a technique often adopted by Pop artists, who typically turned their attention to objects of mass consumption.

ARTISTIC PIRACY

Over and above his activity as an artist, Warhol's boldness and provocativeness were conspicuous traits of his personal life as well: his aspect and behavior never failed to clash drastically with the image of masculinity that his predecessors had carefully fostered. Moreover, unlike them, Warhol consciously attempted to correct, so to speak, the universals of Abstract Expressionism and to "re-Americanize" the art of the United States. In fact, like the phenomenon of Pop art itself, the themes of his work were always thoroughly American.

Pop artists never formed a coherent movement, nor did they issue manifestos or joint formal announcements, and in spite of their common fondness for popular imagery and a shared predilection for commercial artistic techniques, their respective styles were

Jasper Johns. PAINTED BRONZE. 1960. A precursor of Warhol's soup cans, which he began painting two years after this work by Johns.

altogether distinct and unmistakable. When looking at Pop painting, one immediately realizes that its themes are hardly, if ever, original—they are not the product, that is, of the artist's creative imagination. No longer an original creator, the Pop artist merely observes and selects. Pop art is a form of artistic piracy, so to speak. Its thematic choices are based on a repertoire of previously processed images: not a live girl, but a pinup from a magazine; not a real can or package, but the printed ad for a can or a package. Building on the same symbols and themes, Warhol bypassed entirely any type of painterly packaging: instead of presenting merchandise as a sublimated theme, he rendered it with the same crude and exact makeup of advertising; instead of using his own expressive and creative force, he offered a plain reproduction; instead of an individual style, he resorted to the impersonal process of printing.

AN ART FOR ALL

Warhol's aim was to bridge the gap between avant-garde artists and the public. The common people, not the intellectual elite, are the intended recipients of his work. Pop art was meant for everybody, not only for the select few. Warhol wanted to put an end to the stereotype of the artist in an ivory tower; he chose instead to descend into the streets, exhibit his work in shop windows, and appropriate the most typical products of mass consumption. Hence the familiarity of his art; like Pop art in its original formulation, it attempts to react against those elite viewers who had tried to impose one single form of art—and one type of response to it—to the exclusion of all others. In some instances, however, the viewer's response may be different from what Warhol intended, since the layperson is not always likely to grasp the value of his oeuvre. One of the principal characteristics of the Pop artist's work is its transience: as soon as its themes are no longer recognizable for posterity, its interest will for the most part disappear. The novelty and originality of Warhol's art is firmly rooted in its choice of pictorial contents, which, for future generations of viewers, is bound to lose its primitive sense of radical desacralization of traditional myths.

MIDAS'S TOUCH

His transgressive attitude notwithstanding, Warhol managed to gain wide public acceptance and, toward the end of his career, as Benjamin H. D. Buchloh has suggested, he had apparently succeeded in reconciling "the two poles of modernistic dialectic, the department store and the museum." (Indeed, Warhol once claimed that "department stores are kind of like museums.") In 1986, while his works hung in important collections alongside great masterpieces from the past, the artist offered a portrait sitting for sale at 35,000 dollars in the Christmas issue of the Neiman-Marcus mail-order catalog. Like King Midas, Warhol appears to have had the power of turning to gold all that he touched. Even the most insignificant, trite, and cheap object could potentially be converted into a work of art. In modern times, mankind in general and artists in particular appear to have been absorbed by the external world, pushing the inner world of the self into the background. Contemporary society seems fascinated by exactly this type of cynical and transgressive artist

EGG PAINTING, 1982. The Egg Paintings are one of a number of series of virtually abstract paintings that Warhol undertook in the 1980s and which are quite unlike the rest of his oeuvre.

glorified by the media. There appears to be a widespread worship accorded to the artist as businessperson or the businessperson as artist who is able to equate consumerism with a form of egalitarianism: "What's great about this country is that America started the tradition where the richest consumers buy essentially the same things as the poorest. You can be watching TV and see Coca-Cola, and you can know that the President drinks Coke, Liz Taylor drinks Coke, and just think, you can drink Coke too. A Coke is a Coke and no amount of money can get you a better Coke than the one the bum on the corner is drinking. All the Cokes are the same and all the Cokes are good. Liz Taylor knows it, the President knows it, the bum knows it, and you know it."

ANDY WARHOL, 1928–1987

There exists a wealth of information about Andy Warhol, though much of it is contradictory. The artist himself obsessively documented his own existence with a profusion of data and photographs but often omitted or changed facts as he saw fit. The frequently disputed year of his birth is 1928, when, on August 6, he was born Andrew Warhola in Pittsburgh, the youngest of four children of Ondrej and Julia Warhola (the oldest, a girl, died in infancy), Czechoslovakian immigrants who had settled in the Pennsylvanian city. His mother—who lived with him for many years and even collaborated on some of his works—figured prominently in Warhol's childhood recollections. After the death of his father —a coal mine worker—in 1942, the Warholas led an existence of near indigence.

FROM ANDREW TO ANDY

In 1945 Warhol entered the Carnegie Institute of Technology, where he majored in painting and design and received a rather unconventional artistic education. While in school, he worked part-time as a window dresser for a number of department stores, making his earliest contacts with what would become the principal environment of his activity, namely the world of consumption and advertising. In 1948–49 he submitted, as an official entry at the annual show of the Associated Artists of Pittsburgh, his painting *The Broad Gave Me My Face, Butt I Can Pick My Own Nose*, which, after being turned down by the admission committee, was eventually shown in some alternative exhibition space. Even as a boy, Warhol had been intrigued by the possibility of changing his identity, and that work, despite the obvious humor of the title, was evidence of how deeply dissatisfied he was with his own appearance. (In 1950 Warhol began wearing the first of his trademark wigs, and, in 1957, he elected to undergo plastic surgery.)

In the summer of 1949, after graduating from the Carnegie Institute of Technology, Warhol left Pittsburgh for New York in the company of his friend the artist Philip Pearlstein. The move marked the starting point of an entirely new existence: Andrew Warhola died and from his ashes Andy Warhol rose. In New York, he worked as a free-lance commercial artist for such well-known magazines as *Glamour, Vogue, The New Yorker,* and *Harper's Bazaar*; for retail stores such as Tiffany & Co., Bergdorf Goodman, and Bonwit Teller; and, most notably, for the I. Miller shoe company. Thus he achieved

Andy Warhol shopping in a supermarket in 1964. The same year he undertook the series of silkscreens of grocery cartons, including some identical to the Brillo boxes visible in his cart.

a long-coveted financial security. His work began to obtain a certain recognition, and in 1952 his first solo exhibition, "Andy Warhol: Fifteen Drawings Based on the Writings of Truman Capote," was held at an art gallery in Manhattan. This event marked the beginning of a countless series of rewards, and gradually his dreams began to come true.

A RETURN TO PAINTING

After securing a formidable reputation in the advertising world as an illustrator, Warhol in 1960 undertook to change his professional identity from that of commercial artist to practitioner of the fine arts. Among his first efforts upon his return to painting were works in oil with comic strip characters as their theme. To his amazement, in 1961 he found out that another young artist, Roy Lichtenstein, had been working on the same idea, with more successful results. Warhol quickly abandoned his comic-strip paintings.

Just as Warhol's output as an illustrator would eventually infiltrate the art of the avant-garde—with which, unlike the average graphic artist, he was very familiar—his paintings were deeply influenced by such commercial techniques as mass production. In 1961, five of his cartoon paintings were hung as a sort of backdrop in a window display at the Bonwit Teller department store. The following year saw the emergence of some of Warhol's most recognizable themes: the Campbell's Soup cans and the Disasters, as well as the portraits of Elvis Presley and Marilyn Monroe, which marked the beginning of his experimentation with screen-printing techniques.

LEO CASTELLI, 1975. Castelli, one of America's most influential art dealers, played a prominent role in promoting Warhol's work and Pop art in general, both in the United States and in Europe.

At the same time, Warhol was developing a growing interest in films, and in 1963—the year of *Sleep*—he tried his hand at moviemaking. For Warhol, the chief interest of cinema, as well as of photography, lay in its immediacy. Moreover, both techniques required only a minimal intervention on the part of the artist: the real work was done by the camera and the subject.

THE FACTORY

In 1963, Warhol moved his studio to 231 East 47th Street, in what would soon become known as the Factory. Warhol's metamorphosis, and its significance for the history of art, was spectacular: from individual independent artist to head of a factory of art-workers who were able to churn out works as from an assembly line. "The reason I'm painting this way," he once said, "is that I want to be a machine." Aided by his assistants and associates, Warhol proceeded to gather around himself a sort of Renaissance court that enabled him to keep up the high output necessary to meet his financial needs. Nonetheless he always remained open to outside suggestions.

JEAN-MICHEL BASQUIAT, c. 1982. At the time of this portrait, Basquiat was not yet himself world famous as a painter but was simply one of the many figures who made up the peculiar Warholian universe of the Factory. In 1984 he collaborated with Warhol on a series of silkscreens and another of paintings.

More than a mere workplace, the Factory was transformed by theatrical lighting designer Billy Name into a sort of all-encompassing fantasy world of aluminum foil and metallic silver paint. This truly amazing place was visited by all manners of people, from students and young artists to actors, rock stars, and transvestites, and soon the Factory became one of the trendiest gathering places for the "in" crowd and the center of New York's cultural universe.

In 1961 Warhol used five of his own paintings as backdrop for a window display at the Bonwit Teller department store in New York. Art and consumption were always two closely linked concepts in the work of the artist.

Many of the works Warhol based on topical events issued directly from press photographs. This image was the source of the series Race Riots.

The year 1966 marked the beginning of his close collaboration with the musical group The Velvet Underground, as the two staged multimedia "happenings" in New York and California. Two years later, the radical feminist Valerie Solanas shot the artist in an assassination attempt. Severely wounded by the gunshot, which ricocheted in his body, Warhol spent almost two months in the hospital.

A STAR IS BORN

After the 1960s Warhol's output skyrocketed with frequent incursions into virtually every artistic field. Soon his own celebrity began to eclipse that of his portrait subjects, as he traveled in the company of socialites, movie stars, and rock-and-roll stars. Warhol's work from the 1970s and 1980s was of a much more painterly nature than before; his brushwork had become more expressive and visually more complex, adding a certain vitality to the coldness of the silkscreen medium.

His career experienced one final major twist as he turned toward the most abstract works of his entire production with such series as his Oxidation Paintings, Shadows, Egg Paintings, and Threads. On February 22, 1987, following the surgical removal of his gallbladder, Warhol died in a New York hospital. His death marked the end not only of a great artist but of an era. The funeral was held in the artist's native Pittsburgh.

1928 Andy Warhola is born on 6 August in Pittsburgh. His parents are Slovak immigrants from the Carpathians.
Warhol's father arrived in the United States in 1913 but was not rejoined by his wife, Julia, until 1921 because of the First World War.

1934-1935 At a young age, Warhol loves collecting photographs of film stars.

1936-1938 At around the age of nine, Warhol suffers from an attack of St. Vitus' Dance and spends a month recovering in bed, passing the time by filling in coloring books.

1939 He spends a lot of time listening to the radio his parents have just bought.

1942 His father dies.

1945 He enrolls to study pictorial design at the Carnegie Institute of Technology.

1948-1949 Warhol graduates and moves to New York with his friend Philip Pearlstein. *Glamour* is the first to publish his drawings. Later come *Vogue*, *The New Yorker*, *Harper's Bazaar* and others. He Americanizes his surname to Warhol.

1950 He moves. Fritzie Miller becomes his agent.

1952 He is receives the Art Directors Club prize for the best advertising in the press. First solo exhibition at the Hugo Gallery in New York.

1954 He receives a Certificate of Excellence from the American Institute of Graphic Arts. Exhibition at the Loft Gallery, New York.

1956 He is awarded more prizes. He creates collages of shoes using gold leaf. The details of the shoes represent famous personalities. He goes on a round-the-world tour between 16 June and 12 August.

1957 Exhibition at the Bodley Gallery in New York.

1959 Warhol buys a townhouse on Lexington Avenue and moves into it with his mother.

1960 His first canvases depicting comic strip characters.

1961 At the Leo Castelli Gallery, he sees Lichtenstein's paintings inspired by strip cartoons and decides to give up his own work along the same lines.

1962 He begins his major series: *Campbell's Soup*, *Disasters*, *Do-It-Yourself Paintings*, *Elvis* and *Marilyn*. His first silkscreen prints on canvas. His friend Geldzahler brings Rauschenberg to his studio. Solo exhibitions in Los Angeles and at the Stable Gallery in New York.

1963 *Electric Chairs* and *Race Riots*. Warhol buys a 16-mm cine camera and makes his first film. He moves into number 231 on East 47th Street, which he calls the Factory. He begins to wear a platinum blonde wig. He meets Marcel Duchamp, whom he later films.

1964 *Boxes*, *Flowers*, *Most Wanted Men* and *Self-portraits*. He continues to make films and is awarded the Independent Filmmakers' Award by the magazine *Film Culture*. Exhibitions at the Ileana Sonnabend Gallery, the Stable and the Leo Castelli Gallery.

1965 He meets Paul Morrissey, who goes on to play a major role in the Factory's film productions. Numerous exhibitions in the United States and in Italy.

1966 Wallpaper with cow motif, *Self-portraits* and *Silver Clouds*. Exhibition at the Leo Castelli Gallery. Premiere of the film *The Chelsea Girls*: two reels are screened side by side with different sound volumes in the exhibition rooms.

1967 *Electric Chairs*. Numerous films and exhibitions, notably at the Galerie Rudolf Zwirner in Cologne. Warhol shows self-portraits in the United States pavilion at Expo '67 in Montreal.

1968 The Factory moves to 33 Union Square Street. He makes the films *Blue Movie*, also known as *Fuck*, and *Flesh*. Retrospective at the Moderna Museet in Stockholm. On 3 June, Warhol is seriously wounded in an attack by the militant feminist Valerie Solanis. He is admitted to hospital and remains for some time drifting between life and death. He does not leave hospital until 28 July.

1969 He founds the magazine *Interview*. Exhibitions in Berlin and at the Leo Castelli Gallery in New York. He makes the film *Trash*.

1970 Exhibitions, notably at the Pasadena Art Museum, the Musée d'art moderne de la Ville de Paris and the Tate Gallery in London. Warhol shows work at Expo '70 in Osaka.

1971-1972 Numerous exhibitions around the world. Warhol returns to painting, having given it up after the attack. His mother dies. *Warhol Maos* exhibition at the Kunstmuseum, Basel.

1973 He appears in the film *The Driver's Seat* alongside Liz Taylor.

1974 Warhol moves into the townhouse he has just bought on East 66th Street. The Factory moves to 860 Broadway. Exhibition at the Musée Galliera and the Galerie Ileana Sonnabend in Paris. He makes the film *Andy Warhol's Frankenstein*.

1975-1976 His *Skulls* series. Exhibitions around the world. Harcourt Brace Jovanovich publishes *The Philosophy of Andy Warhol (From A to B and back Again)*.

1977-1978 Retrospective in Washington. *Oxidation Paintings*. He makes the film *Andy Warhol's Band*.

1979 Major exhibition at the Whitney Museum of American Art.

1980-1983 *Portraits of Joseph Beuys, Portraits of Jews of the 20th Century* and *Diamond Dust Shoes*.

1984 *Rorschach* series. These paintings, done in collaboration with Jean-Michel Basquiat and Francesco Clemente, are exhibited, notably at the Galerie Bruno Bischofberger in Zurich.

1985 In the Area, a nightclub in New York, Warhol creates an invisible sculpture whose presence is indicated solely by the label. Exhibition of canvases painted in collaboration with Basquiat.

1986 *Camouflages, Flowers, Portraits of Friedrich Der Grosse* and *Self-portraits*. Trip to Paris.

1987 He dies on 22 February following an operation on his gall bladder. He is buried in Pittsburgh. The Andy Warhol Foundation for the Visual Arts is set up with the aim of supporting plastic arts institutions and manifestations.

SUCCES IN NEW YORK

Warhol's first assignment as a commercial artist in New York was a series of illustrations accompanying an article titled "Success Is a Job in New York," which was published in the September 1949 issue of *Glamour*. After this initial success, more jobs flowed in. Shoes first appeared as a theme in Warhol's production in 1955 —as illustrations for a book titled *A la Recherche du Shoe Perdu*— and proceeded to become the most readily identifiable motif of Warhol's early work. A year later, the artist launched what would become his most successful series: the Golden Slippers—realized, for the most part, as gold-leaf collages—were associated with a variety of movie stars and other celebrities. By 1959 Warhol had become an established and celebrated commercial artist. One of the main characteristics of his work from this period was the use of the so-called blotted-line technique, which would become one of his most recognizable trademarks. Warhol had accidentally discovered this technique as a student when, by chance, he applied some blotting paper onto one of his ink drawings: the resulting impression fascinated him because it looked like a reproduction. A primitive form of printing, this technique enabled him to hasten the demise of the traditional distinction between an original and its copies.

A LA RECHERCHE DU SHOE PERDU, 1955. Warhol invented the game—with clearly fetishist connotations—of identifying a specific item of footwear with the person wearing it. In Warhol's work, shoes—a sort of pedestal used by all mortals alike—are no longer just another wardrobe article or an abstract pictorial motif, but an extension or appendage of the individual in their own right. The clumsy manual quality of the image is underscored by the childlike handwriting of the text and signature, probably traced by the artist's mother.

à La Recherche
du Shoe Perdu

by andy Warhol

BABS, 1956. A taste for golden slippers is an indication of power and royalty, which is why they are associated with movie stars and other glamorous celebrities. Warhol "designed" footwear for Elvis Presley and Judy Garland, and in every instance his shoes were works of extreme aesthetic refinement, trimmed with exquisitely fine leaves of gold and silver.

UNTITLED (MAN RIDING A
ROOSTER), *c*. 1957. This naïve
image almost seems excerpted
from a children's story. As a
child, the artist frequently
suffered from bouts of depression
that confined him to bed for
long periods. During his
convalescence, his mother would
read to him a number of tales
that, owing to her difficulty
with the language, were barely
intelligible. In his early
works, Warhol cultivated a
taste for simple and ingenuous
themes, with no more aesthetic
significance than what issues
directly from their technical
execution.

UNTITLED (UNIDENTIFIED MAN), *c.* 1957. One instance of gold-leaf painting combined with the "blotted-line" technique. Throughout his career Warhol devoted a great part of his creative energy to portraiture, although most of his models were well-known celebrities. This picture feels almost like the homework of an art student who, having been assigned the theme of the classical profile, tackled it in a revolutionary manner. The artist has done nothing to conceal from the viewer's gaze the somewhat slapdash joining of the gold leaves with which, imitating the traditional craft of the gilding artist, he decorated this image.

UNTITLED (COSMETICS), 1962. Warhol—one of whose favorite pastimes was visiting department stores—was given to buying large quantities of products of mass consumption, such as bottles of perfume, jars of lotion, shoes, and other items, then using them to create models like this one, which has the unfinished quality of a sketch for an ad for women's cosmetics.

SUPERMAN, 1960. The subject
of this painting was not
particularly innovative, since
his roommate Philip Pearlstein
had already depicted the comic-
book character in 1952, albeit
with expressionistic tones, and
later, between 1958 and 1961,
the same theme was incorporated
into Pop aesthetics by Jasper
Johns, Robert Rauschenberg,
and Roy Lichtenstein. Warhol
may have abdicated iconographic
originality but could not
renounce a personal touch,
as evinced by the traces of
color crayon in the upper
right corner.

ART AS FORMULA

Warhol's career underwent a fundamental change when, in the early 1960s, he decided to give up on his activity as a commercial illustrator to devote himself entirely to the fine arts. For the most part, his works were painted by hand with acrylic paint diluted in water, which allowed them to dry in a short time. As a rule, their themes proceeded from the world of advertising that he recently abandoned and from the mass media. Warhol often led the viewing public to believe that anybody could execute his works and that, as an artist, he acted merely as an intermediary. The paintings of the 1962 series titled *Do It Yourself*—drawing kits for amateurs—are unmistakable evidence of his notion of art as formula, a recipe, as it were, complete with a set of detailed step-by-step instructions. No need to take any chances: just pick your theme, blend in the ingredients in the recommended quantity, and you are guaranteed to succeed. "When I have to think about it," he maintained, "I know the picture is wrong. . . . Some people, they paint abstract, so they sit there thinking about it because thinking makes them feel they're doing something. But my thinking never makes me feel I'm doing anything."

BEFORE AND AFTER, 1960. This work, along with *Advertisement*,
was used as a background decoration of a window, display at
the Bonwit Teller department store in New York. Warhol closely
imitates the images used in authentic ads of this type and limits
his intervention to transferring them onto the canvas with ever-so-
slight technical variations. The underlying idea—venting a personal
complex of the artist—intimates the miraculous outcome of plastic
surgery of the nose, which Warhol himself underwent in 1957. Both
thematically and from a compositional point of view, this picture
is at the origin, of many of his later works.

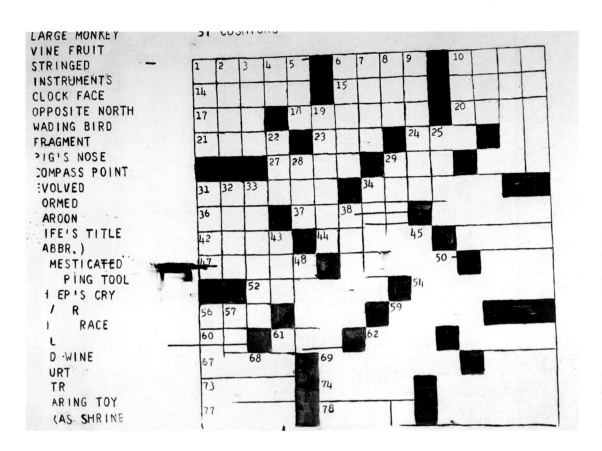

LARGE MONKEY
VINE FRUIT
STRINGED
INSTRUMENTS
CLOCK FACE
OPPOSITE NORTH
WADING BIRD
FRAGMENT
PIG'S NOSE
COMPASS POINT
EVOLVED
ORMED
AROON
IFE'S TITLE
ABBR.)
MESTICATED
PING TOOL
EP'S CRY
/ R
RACE
L
D WINE
URT
TR
ARING TOY
(AS SHRINE

CROSSWORD PUZZLE, 1960. Here Warhol prods viewers to abandon their traditional passivity and take on an active role in the making of the work of art itself. The canvas—as Rauschenberg used to maintain—represents a horizontal plane, and that is just about the only position in which the puzzle can be solved. This particular work is also indebted to the famous paintings of numbers and letters that Johns produced in the mid-1950s.

TELEPHONE, 1961. In this
painting Warhol has
appropriated the taste of
Francis Picabia and other
Surrealist and Dadaist artists
for machinery and mechanical
parts endowed with sexual
connotations. In spite of some
patently hand-painted areas,
the regular, clear-cut edges
give this picture the cold,
industrial look of a printed
image.

UNTITLED (HERNIA), 1960-62. This diagram, an illustration of the
male sexual apparatus, seems taken from a textbook or a medical
reference book, stripped of its explanatory legend with the
corresponding terminology. It is unmistakably reminiscent
of certain Surrealist imagery ad well as of Marcel Duchamp's
ready-mades, even though Warhol's intervention as an artist, by
painting it directly on the canvas, exceeded the mere clipping
and decontextualization of a pre-existing drawing.

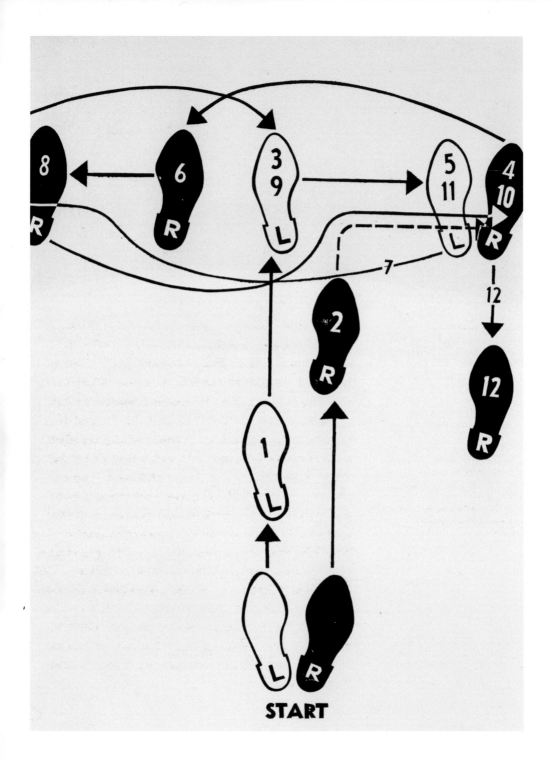

DANCE DIAGRAM (TANGO), 1962.
This image is a black-and-white
reproduction of a diagram from
a handbook that teaches the
steps of ballroom dances.
The artist's intervention is
limited to a shift in scale,
medium, and installation
(from its intended horizontal
placement on the floor to
being displayed vertically on
a wall). Here Warhol followed
the same course as Lichtenstein,
who, the same year had copied
the diagrams from Erle Loran's
book *Cézanne's Composition* into
his own *Portrait of Madame
Cézanne*.

In 1966 Warhol decided to fend off accusations launched against
screen-printing as too mechanical a process and therefore not
applicable to works of art. Warhol had started using this technique
in 1962—it is still unresolved whether he or Rauschenberg was the
first to make use of this medium—because it expedited his work,
but, at the time, he was still not fully aware of all the possibilities
that silkscreen printing could afford. Warhol had originally resorted
to this method for his sketches; in the end, it resulted in his single
most important technical contribution to contemporary painting.
Not only does screen-printing enable the immediate appropriation
of an image, it is an easy-to-use process that is open to unlimited
replication. His earliest silkscreens on canvas are those of the
Dollar Bills series, but he also used the screen-printing technique to
reproduce boxes of Campbell's Soup (avowedly singled out because
it constituted the staple of his daily diet), Heinz ketchup, and Brillo
pads—three products that, through Warhol's work, have achieved
a genuinely iconic status in contemporary civilization. Warhol once
said that "department stores are kind of like museums"; here the
supermarket has been transformed by the artist's whim into a kind
of museum as well.

210 COCA-COLA BOTTLES, 1962
This work is composed of the
consecutive repetitions of
three views of a Coca-Cola
bottle reproduced in a strictly
linear formation. The viewer
is at once aware of color
variations, but only a
closer examination reveals
the differences in the model
itself. What seemed to require
merely a cursory glance demands
instead a detailed observation
if the viewer wishes to
apprehend the significance
of the work in its entirety.

FRONT AND BACK DOLLAR BILLS,
1962. For this series, Warhol
first prepared two silkscreen
plates of a one-dollar bill
by hand and later printed it
on the canvas, albeit not
necessarily in orderly fashion.
Installations of money hanging
on a wall appear to have been
one of the artist's most
characteristic jokes. The
spiritual quest traditionally
associated with the artistic
enterprise is here replaced by
the celebration of monetary
remuneration. Left unresolved
is the question of whether
Warhol's was a cynical posture
or a brutal form of honesty
with regard to the real nature
of art as a commercial
transaction.

100 CAMPBELL'S SOUP CANS, 1962. In 1980 Warhol declared that he wished to be remembered as a soup can, which may very well become the case, since in his work he reiterated time after time precisely that image. One of the *raisons d'être* of this type of work is quite simply the multiplication, the ironic self-plagiarism in a society in wich culture and low-cost products apparently go hand in hand.

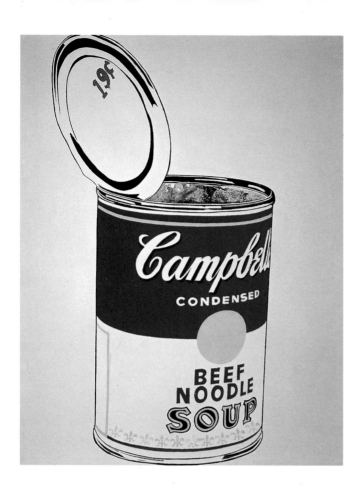

BIG CAMPBELL'S SOUP CAN, 19 CENTS, 1962; CAMPBELL'S SOUP CAN, 1965.
Warhol always introduced slight variations to the original makeup
of the objects that he copied. In the case of the soup cans, he
eliminated the design of the seal impressed in the circle at the
center and sometimes emphasized the lettering with ann additional
border—two procedures the artist employed intentionally, as
confirmed by some of his assistants. There are also, however,
differences between the motifs themselves, and two soup cans are
never identical: their colors change, as does their position;
some are open while others are closed, and some still retain the
price marking, as if they had just been purchased by the artist.

BRILLO BOX (SOAP PADS), 1964; DEL MONTE BOX (PEACH HALVES), 1964.
For his grocery-carton sculptures, Warhol utilized dozens of wooden
crates, which he and his assistants first painted the same color as
the original cartons, then silkscreened on each face a facsimile of
their respective designs. These series tackle the dual issue of
three-dimensional art and of ready-mades. In this case, Warhol's
inspirational sources included both the work of Marcel Duchamp
and Jasper Johns's sculpture *Painted Bronze* (1960).

VARIOUS BOXES, 1964. The interest of this work lies in its theatrical value, since it depends on its artist's ability to adequately arrange the objects in a fitting space more than on the intrinsic qualities of the objects by themselves.

This installation is clearly reminiscent of some typically Minimalist works. During the 1960s, Carl Andre and Robert Morris probed exactly this type of artistic expression, swinging back and forth between two compositional extremes: absolute order and absolute disorder. In the work under examination, Warhol appears to have elected an original and intermediate formula: his boxes—arranged in rows—are sometimes unexpectedly displaced or gently pivoted.

FLOWERS, 1966; COW, 1966.
Thematically, both works are
tuned in to the prevalent
hippie aesthetics of the times.
The first version of the Flowers
series dates from 1964; it arose
from a photograph published in
Modern Photography magazine.
Originally Warhol's idea was
to produce large numbers, in
different colors, of the two
motifs: the flowers on canvas
and the cows on wallpaper. The
conservators of the Whitney
Museum of American Art refused
to consent to the wallpaper's
adhesion directly to the museum's
wall on the occasion of a
retrospective held in 1970.
The final effect would have been
not unlike that of the sweeping
mural paintings of Monet's Water
Lilies.

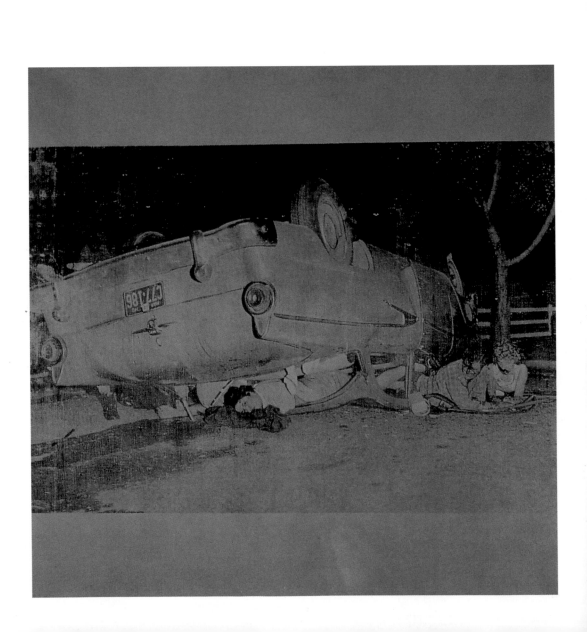

FIVE DEATHS ON ORANGE, 1963.
A turning point in Warhol's
career occurred with the
transition from hand-made
silkscreens to photographic
screen-printing. This
mechanical process—which both
Warhol and Rauschenberg began
using in 1962—consisted of
making silkscreen stencils of
black-and-white photographs
and, in some instances,
retouching them with bright
colors at a later stage.

REPORTS OF DEATH

The other side of American life—the counterpoint to everyday frivolity, that is—are the death-related themes to which Warhol appeared to be strangely but intensely attracted. As a whole, the works in which they appear constitute a sort of documentary chronicle of modern catastrophes, whether acts of God or calamities caused by human intervention. Earthquakes, suicides, plane crashes, automobile accidents, the atomic bomb, and the electric chair are all incorporated into the artist's iconographic repertoire. For the most part, the themes and distinctive layout of these images were directly derived from newspaper articles, whose format was the most effective for this type of motif: in some instances, Warhol even chose to reproduce—with oil paints on canvas—entire newspaper pages, and those paintings ended up looking like ready-mades. In most of them, the artist obsessively repeated the same strangely colored and juxtaposed images, with the result that the viewer is somehow urged to scrutinize and ponder the same tragedy over and over. Warhol's attitude was typical of his age, an era in which the public had become numbly accustomed to the most atrocious horrors. As a chronicler of his time, the artist presents the images unedited: he provides no commentary, the mere selection of a particular image representing his own critical contribution.

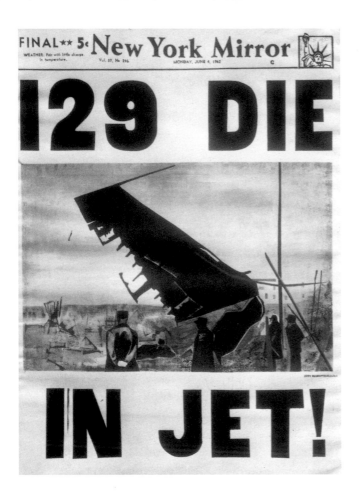

129 DIE IN JET (PLANE CRASH), 1962. While painted entirely by hand, this work is almost an exact reproduction of the first page of a daily newspaper chronicling the dramatic crash of a flight that had originated in the United States while preparing to land at a Paris airport. The disaster had more than a personal resonance; it also marked a cultural and artistic loss, since many of the victims were sponsors of the Atlanta High Museum of Art.

CAR CRASH, 1963. For the most part, Warhol's death-related images are based on press agency photographic material. In some instances, as in the work at hand, the image is tirelessly repeated, since the artist—as he stated in a 1980 interview—believed in quantity rather than quality. The wreckage's heap of mangled strap keeps haunting the viewer's imagination time after time.

LAVENDER DISASTER, 1963. The electric chair as an execution device is—like everything else in Warhol's work—a typically American artifact. The vacant and solitary space is filled only by the chair, which, no longer an object of everyday life, has been transformed into a lethal seat of torture. The lighting tinges the stark hall with a sophisticated mauve tone —the title alludes to Pollock's famous *Lavender Mist*—that assuages the anxiety of the viewers, whom a sign on the right-hand side instructs to remain silent.

SUICIDE, 1963. This spectacular suicide—a jump from the Empire State Building—is one of the few examples of Warhol's work on death in which the actual victim is represented. The subject remains unidentified, but thanks to a singular death, s/he belatedly achieved fame—a macabre instance illustrating one of Warhol's better-known statements: "In the future, everybody will be world famous for fifteen minutes."

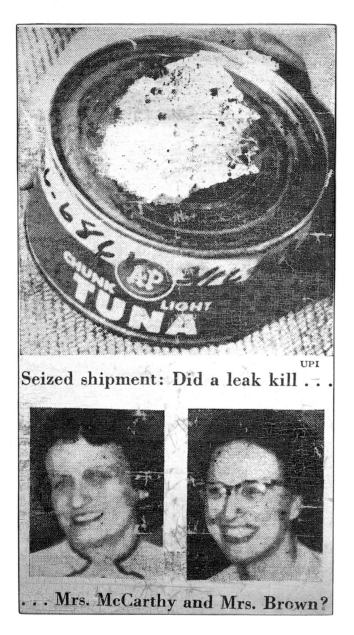

Seized shipment: Did a leak kill . . .

. . . Mrs. McCarthy and Mrs. Brown?

TUNAFISH DISASTER, 1963. The link between mass consumption and death is apparent in the case of these two women who were poisoned by the ingestion of tainted tuna. The black-and-white composition is nearly identical to the original photograph: it even includes the same exact text accompanying the news of the two deaths.

SMALL RACE RIOT, 1964. In spite Warhol's seeming political
neutrality, several of his works drew inspiration from the problems
associated with the racial question in the United States, namely
the uprisings that had been taking place in Birmingham during that
period. These images are genuine denunciations of intolerance,
violence, and brutality. The artist's censure is expressed solely
but powerfully by the striking and bare evidence of the images,
without the further addition of any other form of commentary.

MOST WANTED MEN. NO. 2 JOHN VICTOR G., 1964; MOST WANTED MEN. NO. 2
JOHN VICTOR G., 1964. Don't criminals have a right to be famous?
Warhol designed a large mural for the New York State pavilion at
the 1964 World's Fair with the pictures of thirteen alleged criminals.
The original small photographs were obtained from the archive of the
Federal Bureau of Investigation. Warhol converted them into large
silkscreens, which accounts for the huge dots and graininess of
the images. The installation raised widespread indignation, which
in turn led to the withdrawal of the works and their obliteration
with a coat of silver paint.

ATOMIC BOMB, 1965. Warhol's
intention, with this red-tinted
apocalyptic image, is to
force the viewer to ponder
the subject of death, which
had become his own personal
obsession. The artist tackles
his theme with the same
desensitized moral and
emotional disposition as did
Manet in the latter's versions
of *The Execution of Maximilian*.
Whether one likes them or not,
these paintings by Warhol speak
volumes on the modern condition
of the human race.

SKULL, 1976-77; SKULL, 1976-77.
As far as the use of color is
concerned, these are among
Warhol's boldest compositions.
The skull—a macabre sublimation
of the portrait genre—marks the
culmination of the artist's
series of works on death, while
its continual reiteration may
be seen as a naïve form of
exorcism following the attempt
on his life in 1968.

WARHOL AS COURT PAINTER

Andy Warhol's portraits constitute a genuine gallery of the most influential and famous figures of his age. Politicians, movie stars, and art dealers are among the many names in this long list. None of them was ever chosen by accident: they are all emblems of beauty, glamour, or power; and if that was not the case, Warhol himself made sure they would be transformed into genuine icons through his own work. Even though, for the most part, these celebrities already belonged to the imagery of Pop culture, Warhol's treatment endowed them with a very distinctive quality. He normally first took a snapshot of his subject, then carefully altered it by dislocating the contours and adding new polishes and colors. In many instances, these works are double or multiple portraits, emphasizing the overwhelming presence of their models' already larger-than-life bodies. The ease with which these portraits could be replicated gave a boost to the artist's success and profits, and Warhol never concealed the fact that the genre had become for him an easy moneymaking tool.

MARILYN MONROE'S LIPS, 1962.
Marilyn Monroe's lips are
unquestionably the most erotic
symbol of her widely familiar
features. Thousands of
moviegoers have been affected by
the desire to kiss those lips.
Reduced to a mere anatomical
fragment, Marilyn Monroe is here
converted into a sort of kissing
machine which, ironically,
entails the very dismissal
of the romantic possibility of
a kiss.

TRIPLE ELVIS, 1962. As if in a series of superimposed photographs, this image seems to be moving with suggestive rhythm over a silver background. Warhol obtained this effect with the same type of spray paint used for the bodywork of automobiles. The story of Elvis Presley—a humble youth who, thanks to his music, achieved immense fame and elicited hysterical adoration on the part of young people the world over—is somewhat reminiscent of the artist's own. The other side of the coin, of course, was Elvis's continual bouts of depression and his problems with drugs and alcohol, which led him to a lifelong flirtation with death.

NATALIE, 1962. According to the artist, this tireless repetition
of the gentle features of Natalie Wood—who had recently starred
opposite Warren Beatty in the blockbuster movie *Splendor in the
Grass*—was directly justified by the demands of the viewing public.
Warhol asserted that since moviegoers appear to be interested
only in the image of the star, he chose to repeat that very image
indefinitely. That is the same reason why, in his own films, Warhol
often showed the same actor performing exactly the same action
for hours on end, whether eating, sleeping, or smoking.

SIXTEEN JACKIES, 1964. Like most Americans, Warhol was
profoundly moved by the assassination of the youthful President
John F. Kennedy, on November 22, 1963. One of the consequences
of this tragedy was Jacqueline Kennedy's transformation into
the quintessential widow. Her image, reproduced over and over
in periodicals and on television, traveled throughout the world.
Warhol's series, in which Jackie is shown both smiling and weeping,
is a powerful intimation of how unexpectedly and easily one's lot
can change.

JULIA WARHOLA, 1974. Warhol
painted this portrait of his
mother—undoubtedly the most
influential woman in his life—
two years after she died in
Pittsburgh, at age eighty, after
living with her son in New York
for a number of years. Unlike
most of Warhol's contemporary
portraits, in this one the
sitter's likeness has been,
subjected to hardly any
transformation. The artist's
intervention was limited
to manually retouching the
background and the dress with
very swift brush strokes, which
may explain why this image looks
more like a genuinely painterly
portrait than like a parody.

TRUMAN CAPOTE, 1979. As a young man Warhol had felt a profound admiration for the writer Truman Capote, whose autographs he collected and to whom he once addressed a letter that was left unanswered. In this portrait, Capote is depicted in his element: a public figure with his face brightly lit by the photographers' flashes. As in all of his portraits of celebrities, Warhol underscores some of the model's most prominent features, in this instance his eyes and his hat.

ARCHETYPAL FORMS

Around the 1970s—following a period devoted to a wide variety
of artistic enterprises—Warhol resumed his painterly practice with
renewed enthusiasm. New themes began to emerge in his work
as he started to experiment with an array of new techniques and
mediums. In 1972, he undertook a series of silkscreens titled
Sunset, a nearly abstract image processed through an infinite
number of chromatic variations. His renewed interest in painting
manifested itself above all in his portraits of Mao Ze-Dong. By
emphasizing the most interesting features of the countenance of the
Chinese Communist leader, Warhol's brushwork minimized the most
mechanical aspects of those works while promoting the increasingly
painterly quality of his artistic production. Warhol's evolution as a
painter took him from the sober and bare austerity of the 1960s
—sparing in its colors and harsh in its reliefs—to the most intricate
style, evinced by such traits as the fluid brush strokes and the
imprecise outlines of these portraits. At the same time, the artist's
production experienced a significant iconographic shift: movie stars
began to be replaced by the stars of museums as Warhol decided
to create his own versions of famous paintings. On the other
hand, the archetypal forms recurrent in his works from the 1980s
—the camouflage and Rorschach test series, that is—verge on
pure abstraction, and therefore look back to the farthest origins
of his career.

LADIES AND GENTLEMEN, 1975; LADIES AND GENTLEMEN, 1975. The artist's
manipulation of these images is such that the models' features
retain only a mere echo of their likenesses as seen in the original
photographs. The resulting portraits possess a certain melancholic
quality and are blurred by the successive accumulation of paint.
Both portraits belong to a series devoted to African-American
transvestites that was shown in its entirety only in Europe.

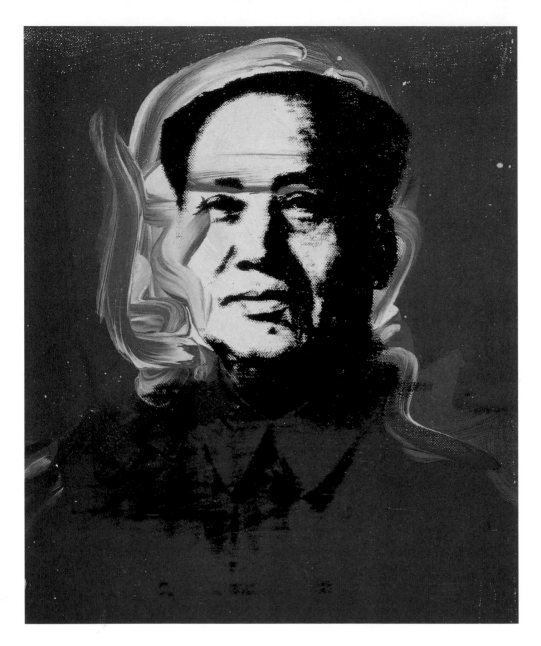

MAO, 1973; MAO, 1973. As a consequence of the student rebellion movement of 1968, Mao became an idol of the younger generations in the West and, paradoxically so, was transformed into a fashionable icon of capitalist society.

Then, in 1972, President Nixon made an unprecedented official trip to China. Soon enough, the Chinese Communist leader joined the movie stars among the cohort of models portrayed by Warhol, and, like theirs, his likeness was replicated inexpensively

only to be sold later like any other commodity. Mao's presence among those more glamorous celebrities does not in any way indicate a form of political commitment on the part of the artist.

OXIDATION PAINTING, 1978; OXIDATION PAINTING, 1978. The technique with which these paintings were executed involved priming the canvas with a blend of synthetic polymer and metal dust and urinating over it while the priming coat was still fresh: the paint surface turned green in different shapes depending on where it had been attacked by the bodily fluid. The process is reminiscent of Jackson Pollock's drippings: a sublimated emulation, that is, of those works in which that artist let the paint trickle over the canvas. In addition to urine, Warhol used for paintings in this series other unconventional materials, such as melted chocolate, strawberry jam, and semen.

JOSEPH BEUYS, 1980.
The glittering effect of the powdered crystal over the model's heat becomes a sort of sacred halo surrounding the head of the German artist who, in this portrait by Warhol, is seemingly transformed into a holy image. Perhaps surprisingly, Warhol had indeed retained a Catholic devoutness from his childhood, and used to pay a daily visit to the church of St. Vincent Ferrer

SIXTY LAST SUPPERS, 1986.
During his last years, Warhol
undertook to produce his personal
interpretation of some of the
most emblematic religious works
of European painting, such as
Leonardo da Vinci's *Last Supper*
and *Annunciation*, or Raphael's
Sistine Madonna. Sometimes these
old masterpieces are quoted in
their entirety while at other
times they are only partially
reproduced. In some instances—
such as the one under
consideration—the original

composition is subjected to
the same process of serial
replication as Warhol's
portraits and advertising
images. The large format of
some of these works is an
allusion to the mural paintings
and altarpieces found in
religious edifices.

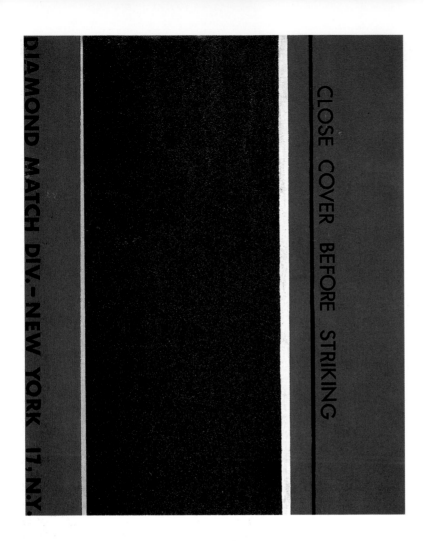

CLOSE COVER BEFORE STRIKING, 1962. This straightforward reproduction of the bottom part of a matchbox is a parody of the paintings by Barnett Newman, whose style was based on the use of a empty fields of saturated color bounded by asymmetrically arranged narrow bands. Warhol undermines the impact that such an immense chromatic continuum has on the viewer by inserting a sign that warns not to light matches before closing the cover. The stripe of sandpaper mimics the rough texture of the scraper against which matches are struck in order to light them.

THE DISQUIETING MUSES (AFTER DE CHIRICO), 1982. The early 1980s saw
the rise of a passionate revisionist interest in De Chirico's late
production. The Italian artist had for the longest time been accused
of having "forged" his own works by dating to an earlier period
paintings that he had actually executed at some later time. Warhol,
who had been charged with plagiarism throughout his entire career,
once more challenged artistic conventions when he produced replicas
of his own copies of the works by the Italian master.

CAMOUFLAGE SELF-PORTRAIT, 1986.
Warhol produced self-portraits
during the entire course of
his artistic career. The
narcissistic hero of this genre
depicts himself with feigned
modesty, assuming the roles
of both viewer and object of
spectacle, at once actor
and spectator. The use
of the military technique of
camouflage—a heritage of his
old fascination with disguises—
successfully conceals and
obscures more than ever the
shy and evasive presence of
the artist and his personality.

p 6

Self-Portrait, 1966.
Acrylic paint and silkscreen ink on
canvas, 55.9 × 55.9 cm

p 19

A la Recherche du Shoe Perdu,
1955.
Offset lithography, watercolor, and
pen nib on paper, 66.4 × 50.8 cm..
Andy Warhol Foundation for the
Visual Arts, Inc.

p 20

Babs, 1956.
Ink, collage, and silver and gold leaf
on paper, 30.5 × 40.6 cm.
Private collection.

p 21

Untitled (Man Riding a Rooster),
c. 1957.
Ink and gold leaf on paper,
50.8 × 36.2 cm.
Private collection.

p 22

Untitled (Unidentified Man), c. 1957.
Ink and gold leaf on paper,
50.8 × 40.6 cm.
Private collection.

p 23

Untitled (Cosmetics), 1962.
Graphite, pastel, and photographic
assemblage on paper; 73.3 × 40.6 cm.
Whereabouts unknown.

p 24

Superman, 1960.
Acrylic and crayon on canvas,
170 × 133 cm.
Private collection, Paris.

p 26

Before and After, 1960.
Acrylic on canvas, 137.2 × 177.8 cm.

p 27

Crossword Puzzle, 1960.
Acrylic on canvas, 112.6 × 160 cm.
Private collection.

p 28

Telephone, 1961.
Acrylic and graphite on canvas,
182.9 × 137.2 cm.

p 29

Untitled (Hernia), c. 1960-62.
Acrylic on canvas, 137.2 × 182.9 cm.
Andy Warhol Museum, Pittsburgh.
Founding Collection, contribution the
Andy Warhol Foundation for the
Visual Arts, Inc.

p 30

Dance Diagram (Tango), 1962.
Acrylic paint on canvas,
181.1 × 132.1 cm.
Andy Warhol Museum, Pittsburgh.
Founding Collection, contribution the
Andy Warhol Foundation for the
Visual Arts, Inc.

pp 32–33

210 Coca-Cola Bottles, 1962.
Acrylic and silkscreen ink on canvas,
208.3 × 266.7 cm.
Private collection, Los Angeles.

p 34

Front and Back Dollar Bills, 1962.
Silkscreen ink on canvas, two panels,
each 210.8 × 48.2 cm.
Private collection, New York.

p 35

100 Campbell's Soup Cans, 1962.
Acrylic on canvas, 182.9 × 132.1 cm.
Albright-Knox Art Gallery, Buffalo.
Gift of Seymour H. Knox.

p 36

Big Campbell's Soup Can, 19 Cents,
1962.
Acrylic and graphite on canvas,
182.9 × 138.4 cm.
The Menil Collection, Houston.

p 37

Campbell's Soup Can, 1965.
Acrylic and silkscreen ink on canvas,
90.4 × 61.6 cm.

p 38

Brillo Box (Soap Pads), 1964.
Silkscreen ink on wood,
43.5 × 43.5 × 35.6 cm.
Andy Warhol Foundation for the
Visual Arts, Inc.

p 38

Del Monte Box (Peach Halves),
1964.
Silkscreen ink on wood,
24.1 × 38.1 × 30.5 cm.
Andy Warhol Foundation for the
Visual Arts, Inc.

p 39

Various Boxes, 1964.
Silkscreen ink on wood, varying
dimensions.

p 40

Flowers, 1966.
Acrylic and silkscreen ink on canvas,
101.6 × 101.6 cm.

p 41

Cow, 1966.
Silkscreen ink on wallpaper,
115.5 × 75.6 cm.

p 42

Five Deaths on Orange, 1963.
Acrylic and silkscreen ink on canvas,
76.2 × 76.2 cm.

p 44

129 Die in Jet (Plane Crash), 1962.
Acrylic on canvas,
254 × 182.9 cm.
Museum Ludwig, Cologne.

p 45

Car Crash, 1963.
Acrylic and silkscreen ink on canvas,
266.7 × 205.7 cm.

p 46

Lavender Disaster, 1963.
Acrylic and silkscreen ink on canvas,
269.2 × 208 cm.
The Menil Collection, Houston.

p 47

Suicide, 1963.
Acrylic and silkscreen ink on canvas,
228.6 × 200.7 cm.

p 48

Tunafish Disaster, 1963.
Acrylic and silkscreen ink on canvas,
104.1 × 55.9 cm.

p 49

Small Race Riot, 1964.
Acrylic and silkscreen ink on canvas,
76.2 × 83.8 cm.
Private Collection.

p 50

**Most Wanted Men, No. 2, John
Victor G.,** 1964.
Silkscreen ink on canvas,
123.2 × 98.1 cm.
Dia Art Foundation, New York.

p 50

**Most Wanted Men, No. 2, John
Victor G.,** 1964.
Silkscreen ink on canvas,
123.2 × 94 cm.
Dia Art Foundation, New York.

p 51

Atomic Bomb, 1965.
Acrylic and silkscreen ink on canvas,
264.1 × 204.5 cm.
Saatchi Collection, London.

p 52
Skull, 1976-77.
Acrylic and silkscreen ink on canvas,
38.1 × 48.3 cm.

p 53
Skull, 1976-77.
Acrylic and silkscreen ink on canvas,
38.1 × 48.3 cm.

p 54
Turquoise Marilyn, 1964.
Acrylic on canvas,
101.6 × 101.6 cm.
Private Collection.

pp 56–57
Marilyn Monroe's Lips, 1962.
Acrylic and silkscreen ink on canvas,
two panels: 210.2 × 205.1 cm;
211.8 × 210.8 cm.
Hirshhorn Museum and Sculpture
Garden, Smithsonian Institution,
Washington, D. C. Gift of Joseph
H. Hirshhorn.

p 58
Triple Elvis, 1962.
Silkscreen ink and aluminum paint
on canvas, 208.3 × 152.4 cm.
Virginia Museum of Fine Arts,
Richmond. Gift of Sydney and
Francis Lewis.

p 59
Natalie, 1962.
Silkscreen ink on canvas,
212.1 × 231.1 cm.
Andy Warhol Museum, Pittsburgh.
Founding Collection, contribution the
Andy Warhol Foundation for the
Visual Arts, Inc.

pp 60–61
Sixteen Jackies, 1964.
Acrylic and silkscreen ink on canvas,
overall 203.2 × 162.6 cm.
Walker Art Center; Minneapolis. Art
Acquisition Fund.

p 62
Julia Warhola, 1974.
Acrylic and silkscreen ink on canvas,
101.6 × 101.6 cm.
Andy Warhol Museum, Pittsburgh.
Founding Collection, contribution the
Andy Warhol Foundation for the
Visual Arts, Inc.

p 63
Truman Capote, 1979.
Acrylic and silkscreen ink on canvas,
101.6 × 101.6 cm.
Dia Art Foundation, New York.

p 64
Marlon Brando, 1966.
Silkscreen ink on canvas,
104.1 × 120 cm.

p 66
Ladies and Gentlemen, 1975.
Acrylic and silkscreen ink on canvas,
35.6 × 27.9 cm.
Andy Warhol Foundation for the
Visual Arts, Inc.

p 67
Ladies and Gentlemen, 1975.
Acrylic and silkscreen ink on canvas,
35.6 × 27.9 cm.
Andy Warhol Museum, Pittsburgh.
Founding Collection, contribution the
Andy Warhol Foundation for the
Visual Arts, Inc.

p 68
Mao, 1973.
Acrylic and silkscreen ink on canvas,
30.5 × 25.4 cm.

p 69
Mao, 1973.
Acrylic and silkscreen ink on canvas,
66 × 55.9 cm.

p 70
Oxidation Painting, 1978.
Mixed mediums on canvas,
101.6 × 76.2 cm.
Andy Warhol Foundation for the
Visual Arts, Inc.

p 70
Oxidation Painting, 1978.
Mixed mediums on canvas,
101.6 × 76.2 cm.
Andy Warhol Foundation for the
Visual Arts, Inc.

p 71
Joseph Beuys, 1980.
Silkscreen ink on paper with
diamond dust, 111.8 × 76.2 cm.

pp 72–73
Sixty Last Suppers, 1986.
Acrylic and silkscreen ink on canvas,
294.6 × 998.2 cm.
Leo Castelli Gallery, New York.

p 74
Close Cover Before Striking, 1962.
Acrylic, Prestype, and sandpaper
on canvas, 40.6 × 50.8 cm.

p 75
**The Disquieting Muses
(After De Chirico),** 1982.
Acrylic and silkscreen ink on canvas,
127 × 106.7 cm.
Andy Warhol Foundation for the
Visual Arts, Inc.

pp 76–77
Camouflage Self-Portrait, 1986.
Acrylic and silkscreen ink on canvas,
203.2 × 203.2 cm.

SELECTED BIBLIOGRAPHY

Alloway, Lawrence. *American Pop
Art.* New York: Collier Books in
association with the Whitney
Museum of American Art, 1974.

*Andy Warhol Collection, The: Sold
for the Benefit of the Andy Warhol
Foundation for the Visual Arts.* 6
vols. New York: Sotheby's, 1988.

Andy Warhol: Death and Disasters.
Houston: Menil Collection and
Houston Fine Arts Press, 1988.

Bockris, Victor. *The Life and Death
of Andy Warhol.* New York: Bantam
Books, 1989.

Bourdon, David. *Warhol.* New York:
Abrams, 1989.

Crone, Rainer. *Andy Warhol.* New
York: Praeger, 1970.

McShine, Kynaston, editor. *Andy
Warhol: A Retrospective.* New York:
The Museum of Moderns Art, 1989.

Ratcliff, Carter. *Andy Warhol.* New
York: Abbeville Press, 1983.

Warhol, Andy. *The Philosophy of
Andy Warhol (From A to B and Back
Again).* New York: Harcourt Brace
Jovanovich, 1975.

Warhol, Andy, and Pat Hackett.
POPism: The Warhol Sixties. New
York: Harcourt Brace Jovanovich,
1980.